What goes up mus
This is because of g

Gravity is a force that pulls things down, like leaves from a tree and rain from the sky.

Gravity is also what makes you slide down a slide, and liquid pour down from a pitcher.

Curves can help slow down the effects of gravity. Otherwise, gravity would pull us straight down very fast.

Gravity is also a force that makes things balance. You balance when your weight is equal on all sides.

You lose your balance when your weight is no longer spread evenly.

And then the force of
gravity pulls you down.

Other forces control movement, too. We move because of the energy in our bodies.

Sailboats and kites move because the force of the wind pushes them.

Cars, trains, and airplanes move because of the fuel we put in them.

Can you tell which energy or force is making the things in these pictures move?

But don't forget the force of gravity.
Because of gravity, we can balance . . .

and be certain that when we go up,
we will always come down.